THE 3 BUCKET METHOD

FOR THE TRUCKING INDUSTRY

Your Best Protection Against Nuclear Verdicts

Joseph Michael Dickerson, J.D., M.B.A.

Marigold Horizon

2 Lindenwood Dr.
Laredo, Texas 78045

The 3 Bucket Method for The Trucking Industry: Your Best Protection Against Nuclear Verdicts
Published by Marigold Horizon
2 Lindenwood Dr.
Laredo, Texas 78045

For more information about our books, please write to us, call 956-791-5422 or visit our website at www.dickersonlaw.com/contact

ISBN-13: 978-1-7332567-5-9

Dickerson, Joseph Michael, 1969-
The 3 Bucket Method for The Trucking Industry: Your Best Protection Against Nuclear Verdicts
Joseph Michael Dickerson.

ISBN-13: 978-1-7332567-5-9
Copyright © 2023 The J.M. Dickerson Law Firm PLLC

The 3 Bucket Method
For Asset Protection
For The Trucking Industry

The 3 Bucket Method
For Asset Protection
For The Trucking Industry

Why The 3 Bucket Method for The Trucking Industry?

If you drive down almost any highway or interstate, you will see the attorney billboards that all ask the same question: “Have you been injured in a trucking accident?” Or some variation of this advertisement. Billboards are not the cheapest form of advertising, so that means that these attorneys are making a lot of money from these cases. Trucking companies have a target on their backs. Trucking companies are sued even if their drivers were not at fault. The attorneys paint the story of big truck versus little car, to gain sympathy from a jury. Once they have success, they use that to try to get the insurance company to settle for a big payoff.

Since 2016, in Texas (and likely throughout the United States) there has been a spread of what we call “Nuclear Verdicts”. These Nuclear Verdicts are judgements in an amount that would wipe out a company due to the size of verdict. In 2016 it started at $35,000,000.00; and these have steadily increased throughout the years. The highest of these so far was in 2018 at $260,000,000.00. It is these extraordinary verdicts that can financially devastate a Trucking Company owner, as the insurance will not be sufficient to cover the judgement.

In 2019 I shared my proven strategies for protecting your assets in my book, *The 3 Bucket Method for Asset Protection.* That book provides a step-by-step strategy that can be employed to protect your assets and keep what you have accumulated from your hard work. The 3 Bucket Method book was designed as a tool to help anyone organize their businesses and assets to insure the maximum protection from lawsuits and other liabilities. I have also given several talks explaining our method to groups and the public in general. I have shared my knowledge with realtors, clients, and members of the Laredo Motor Carriers Association (LMCA).

From my involvement in the LMCA and my work with clients in the transportation industry, I realized that the transportation industry had some specific strategies that fit squarely in The 3 Bucket Method system. I wanted to share a more specific focus to protect owners in this industry.

I have written this book so that it explains and expands on the original 3 Bucket Method without the need to have read the other book first. I will reference my other books throughout for further reading and detail.

I hope that you will find value in this book, whether you are just thinking about entering the industry, are just starting the process of getting your MC and DOT permits or are a seasoned trucking company owner. This book will give you insights and a guide on how you can protect your assets and keep them protected to the maximum extent possible.

If you need our assistance in evaluating your structure, or in setting up your business, we are happy to be of service. I have created a special email to answer your questions from this book:
3BMTruckBook@dickersonlaw.com

I look forward to hearing from you and being of service to you in this adventure.

Foreword

By Raul Garza, CPA, MPA, DABFA

It is an honor and delight to write the foreword to this book on asset protection for the trucking industry written by my esteemed colleague and friend Joseph Michael Dickerson. I consider

Mike to be a great professional, human being, son, husband, father, friend, and God-fearing man. I met Mike in 1998 as a young professional when our careers were in their infancy. By way of introduction, my name is Raul Garza, I am a certified public accountant and have been practicing public accountancy since 1990.

Our practices are situated in Laredo, TX. Laredo is the largest city in Webb County and the county seat. Laredo has historically been one of the fastest growing cities in Texas. It has consistently been a significant part of international trade as the biggest inland port in the U.S. and in the recent years it has become the country's No. 1 international trade port overall, beating larger cities like Chicago, Illinois and Los Angeles, California. My practice has extensive experience in representing clients in the transportation industry. The transportation industry is very fragmented in the USA and has unique intricacies particularly the trucking companies operating in the border cities which have a significant element of international tax issues as some of the owners are Mexican nationals. Throughout the years, Mike and I have advised many clients in the trucking industry for both US citizens and foreign nationals, and it is through this experience that I came to value and respect his work, experience, and professional demeanor as an attorney.

What differentiates Mike from most attorneys is that he has a strong understanding of business, maintains current with changes in the law and takes a very personal and respectful approach to servicing the clients he represents. He understands and values the knowledge and expertise of the tax certified public accountant and how important it is to work as a team for the benefit of the client. It is common to see attorneys take an approach of being infallible, and having inflated personal feelings of personal ability that prohibits them from consulting with other professionals on matters outside of their field of expertise and for the benefit of the client. Mike understands the importance of addressing the civil and tax laws as they work hand in hand and have a major impact on the decisions regarding types of entities used for business planning of any industry.

The following two biblical scriptures best describe Mike's virtues. Proverbs 1:2-3 "To know wisdom and instruction, to understand words of insight, to receive instruction in wise dealing, in righteousness, justice, and equity" and Proverbs 20:3 "Avoiding a fight is a mark of honor; only fools insist on quarreling." Mike is a mild mannered intellectual.

While writing this foreword, I had a course of meetings with three different attorneys and our mutual clients. I had not previously worked with two of these attorneys. One of the attorneys was at the dawn of his career, the second attorney was at the midpoint and the third was at the culmination of his profession in his early 80s. Even though these three attorneys were at the different lifecycles of their careers and obviously went to law school at different decades, they shared a commonality in attitudes as described earlier.

The first two attorneys shared an adamant conviction that there was no difference between a corporation and a limited liability company. Obviously completely ignoring the legal benefits of a charging order protection offered by states like Texas. The third attorney advised our mutual client to create a limited liability company, transfer real estate property then assign the membership units to the children of our mutual client. He was stubborn in recognizing that his planning caused a reportable and taxable transaction by gifting the membership units to the client's children. He erroneously claimed that it was not a gift but rather an assignment of membership units and that it was not necessary to have a valuation of the membership units or the real estate.

I like this book and highly recommended it because Mike takes a very practical and pragmatic approach in explaining the legal, tax and business concepts and emphasizing the importance of proper planning to mitigate the risks inherent to the transportation industry and the needs of the distinct phases of the life of the entrepreneur. He goes on to provide insightful areas that are critical and particular to transportation entrepreneurs. Furthermore, he not only identifies the typical liability risks such as accidents but expands on tax issues that apply to this industry and in the USA. This information is an invaluable source of data for any business owner.

Raul Garza, CPA, MPA, DABFA

Garza Accounting Professionals, PLLC

Certified Public Accountants and Business Advisors
raul@gap-cpa.com

INTRODUCTION

"The creation of a thousand forests is in one acorn." -Ralph Waldo Emerson, American Essayist

Keep in mind the effort it takes to keep your business running smoothly, without floating payroll, stalking the mailbox for clients' checks, or pulling funds from other stashes just to be sure your month is covered. This type of effort is typically what a lot of us sometimes do just to get by. As the saying goes, "it happens," but there IS a way to have mastery of all of the moving parts in your business and in your life. You just need to get a hold of the right "buckets" to contain and protect your most special assets. These buckets embody my philosophy, which I share with my clients when we do their asset protection and estate planning. I call it the 3 Bucket Method for Asset Protection and have specifically tailored it to the trucking industry.

I will explain how, by using the 3 Bucket Method, we identify different business opportunities and strategically separate risk into the three buckets. In addition to the 3 Bucket Method, there will be other items to include in your plan that greatly enhance your asset protection mix, or as my wife likes to call it, your total asset health. I will explore the need for insurance that helps cover the cost of the lawyers who can defend you when dreadful things happen and provide funds to make right any unintended damages. The beauty of this method is that they all work together, they can go into play all at once, or you can grow into them and bring them online one at a time as your trucking business grows.

Part of the reason I wrote this book is because a lot of trucking company owners don't realize the magnitude of risk exposure, they put themselves in just by operating their business day-to-day. Some people are unfortunately one lawsuit away from getting wiped out because they're a sole proprietor or have all of their assets in the same operating business. Basically, as a sole proprietor, the owner and the business are one and the same. There is no separate business entity that protects them; or if they do have an entity, nine times out of ten they don't have their documentation up to date. They use the company checkbook like a personal checkbook. They don't have a record of corporate or LLC minutes documenting different transactions. They don't account for any transactions in their minutes, or anywhere for that matter, and that's the way they handle it. That creates a huge risk of exposure in a lawsuit.

In a lawsuit, the first thing the opposing attorneys are going to ask for is to see your corporate or company book and the last three years of company tax returns. How are you going to answer those questions in a way that doesn't give them a lot of ammunition to use against you? What can you do to make sure that you are okay, and that you are not intimidated by the multitude of TV lawyers looking for their next lucrative case to profit from? Why put yourself in a position where you are worried about somebody wanting to sue you, create a problem, or take what you have worked so hard to build?

The reality is that a lawsuit is going to follow you or your company until you pay it off or go into bankruptcy. And guess what? When you die, the lawsuit is going to go after your estate; and if you have amassed anything, the lawyers and those suing you are going to want to get their cut. The bottom line is you will end up paying now or paying later.

The advantage of employing the 3 Bucket Method is that you can set yourself up in a way that will *actually* protect you in the very scary business environment that is the trucking industry. You ARE going to be able to weather the storms of life. You ARE going to be able to move forward and not be personally tied to the adverse times of life forever. Your assets will be able to continue producing revenue for you. Remember, the business entity can suffer the loss and die; there goes the liability, and you are in a safe zone. You subsequently move on, and you do that by making sure that you've created the right asset protection structures.

Next, you need to MAINTAIN those protection structures. If you don't have company minutes for each year of operation that document the transactions of the company, <u>you are at risk</u>. If you don't have a record in your company book of the different intercompany loans, especially those that require different kinds of tax treatment, you are at risk.

Let me provide an analogy for entity maintenance that I know you will be able to relate to. Imagine you have a brand-new truck. It has your company logo on it and all the DOT and MC numbers, and you get it on the road. It will start to produce and work for you, which is great. But now, what if you don't change the oil, keep the right pressure in the tires, add DEF (Diesel Exhaust Fluid), or even wash the truck? Pretty soon it will be a BRICK that will not move or produce for you. On the contrary, in the trucking industry it will be a liability to have a truck out of service like that. It is the same way with your entity. If you fail to keep up the maintenance, you will be in a situation in which the entity may not provide the protection it was designed to provide when you formed it.

It can get extremely expensive to hire your CPA and attorney to help you retrace your business' steps and create the correct documentation that meets the exacting standards of the IRS for the years your record keeping fell through the cracks. You may not have ANY intercompany agreements and minutes in place. Do you want to open up a window of opportunity in which one of these ambulance-chasing lawyers can probe into your business? I can hear them now. "Hey! These two companies don't even act like they are two separate companies. Why would these separate companies lend money to each other without a promissory note? Why would they let this person have their office on that property without paying rent or having a contract?" Then all of a sudden, there is a jury that appears and says, "Hey! You know what? That makes sense," and the jury has the right to believe they are the same person, especially when you have the same owners and no documentation about their separateness.

That is a risky way to do business. You are only opening up your weaknesses, and in a lawsuit, there's a lot of ways in which the opposing legal team can chip away at the armor of your business structure, especially when you have let it rust from lack of upkeep. It's in your power to keep up the integrity of that armor.

We can certainly create the Cadillac or Mercedes system of protection. But like owning a Cadillac or Mercedes, if you don't change the oil regularly, check the tire pressure and other aspects of routine maintenance, eventually that car can break down, and inevitably at the most inopportune time.

The same can be said of your business. If you don't have your business set up properly and up to date, it is likely you will find out at the worst possible time. You will say to yourself, “If I had only done these things, I would be in a better position to negotiate with strength.”

Wouldn’t you want to say, “Hey, take whatever the insurance company is offering you because you're not getting more than that from me!” Do you want to negotiate from a position of weakness in which all of your separate companies are collapsing, and the opposing side is ready to take it all? You don't want to be in a position where you are asking, "How much can I give you for you to not take all my property away?" These are the things of trucking business owners' nightmares, and scary things can and do happen to the unprepared.

The 3 Bucket Method is a proven method. My clients have used it, I use it myself for my personal investments, and we have used it very successfully. I do what I tell you to do, and I tell you to do what I do. The only requirement: you have to commit in order to maintain it. And I do this too.

So, have you asked yourself the right questions? Do you want to be informed and prepared? Do you want to be on the right path to sustained wealth? Do you want to be in a position where one unintended mistake or accident caused by an employee could cost you your whole livelihood because of a lawsuit? Have you considered having to start from the ground up again? Do you have the energy or resources to start again from scratch? Lastly, do you want to put yourself in a position where you lose all of your hard-earned business assets to lawyers hired by your heirs who are in turn fighting over your assets?

Believe me, the lawyers are eager to get their chunk; and the more they get, the less is available for your heirs to divide. Do you want your assets to be available for your use for as long as you need them and beyond? Do you want to make sure that your legacy to generational wealth is fully paved with a direct route to provide for more than one lifetime? Having an estate plan is a key component to total asset health while protecting your family from disharmony. It can be heartbreaking to see the way the family unit unravels and the polarizing effects of fighting for money. I plan to share with you my philosophy and how I protect my clients from terrible things that can, and in many cases do, happen.

The 3 Bucket Method consists of The Moving Parts Bucket (for operation successes), The Dirt Bucket (for real estate) and the Paper Bucket (for your liquid assets and ownership interests). You will need to have proper insurance in place and an estate plan or succession plan for your assets.

It is important to make sure that the fruits of your success don't just end with you. Your wealth should continue onto your next generation or to the people you want to take over your businesses or continue to provide for your family. Do you want to provide a Legacy for your family? The first strategy we call The Moving Parts Bucket.

SECTION ONE

Entity Structures

Before I discuss the Buckets, it is important to understand the entities that are available in your tool kit. I go into further detail on the types of entities available in my first book, *The Road Map To Rich; a Lawyers Perspective on Getting and*

Staying Rich. I will take this opportunity here to go over the basic forms of business entities that are available to you.

Allow me to focus on Texas, because that's where I'm licensed to practice, but these concepts are fairly universal, so check with your legal advisor in your state.

Sole Proprietor

In Texas, you can do business as a sole proprietor, which means you don't have a business entity, but instead, you the owner and the business are one and the same. This business set up can go badly if things don't go well; an adverse judgment can follow you way past the moment you pay it. The negative effects will keep stalking you forever. This can make your life difficult, especially if the other side's attorneys are really aggressive.

General Partnership

Another form of business is a general partnership, which means you and one or more persons decided to go into business together, but you didn't want to take the time or make the expense of forming an entity. And with the powers of mathematics, all you have managed to do is multiply the risk by the number of partners involved. So, if one of you is the money partner and the other is the sweat equity partner, and a lawsuit springs up, guess who they're going to go after first? That's right, the money partner. The sweat equity partner will be on the hook, but when you don't have anything to lose, there's nothing for them to go after.

Corporation

The next form of business may be something that more people are familiar with, a corporation. Corporations are entities that provide a separation of management and ownership.

The way the Corporation works looks like this: you have your shareholders who are the owners of the business and as owners, shareholders don't have the liability if/when anything goes wrong within the Corporation, so they're protected from any risk that is associated with the operation of the business. A Corporation allows for providing professional management that can make decisions about the business, yet they don't necessarily own any of the business. This benefit provides some risk protection to the owner or owners. Corporations have another thing going for them, in that they've been around for a long time. Over one hundred years, actually, and there's a lot of history on how the courts interpret the bylaws and not the Corporation and the state statutes. In a nutshell, there's a substantial knowledge base of understanding on how Corporations work for your business. The problem with Corporations lies in how we pay taxes within a corporation. As of the writing of this book, Corporations can only pay taxes in one of two ways. When your entity is a C-corporation, the company pays its own taxes and gets a deduction for employee expenses but not deductions for dividends that are paid out as profits to owners. Keep in mind, although it provides protection for the owners from what happens in the business, it doesn't really protect the business from what the owners do. This goes back to our charging order situation. There isn't a charging order statute for Corporations. In other words, if you own a corporation and you personally get sued, they can get a judgment against you, take the shares of your corporation, and liquidate them. In Texas, the Corporation is given a 21-day notice to turn over your shares if you don’t pay off the judgement within the time allowed.

Effectively, the result is the person who sued you has now taken over your ownership. And if you've got partners, guess who the new partner in the corporation is? It's the person who sued your business partner. That's a clear weakness of a corporation.

Limited Liability Company (LLC)

The next form of business is a more popular business entity structure. It's called the limited liability company, or LLC. The LLC has a shorter history than the Corporation. There are some notable differences and similarities between the two. Unlike a Corporation, the owners are called members and the managers who run the business are called managers. Like a Corporation, it separates management and ownerships and offers the same protection, where the owners are not liable for anything that happens in the business. But the difference is, in the LLC, if an owner is sued and there is a judgment against them, the only thing that can remedy this is a charging order against them. A charging order is an order from the court that issued the judgment rendered that says, "LLC, if you make a distribution to Mr. Gonzalez, you have to make it to Mr. Jones who won the lawsuit and has judgment". Well, in the LLC, we are not required to make distributions. Those who have set up their business entity in the LLC, and have the proper language in their company agreements, don't have to make distributions to ANYBODY and have protected themselves in that manner. This is what makes the LLC a popular business entity structure. Another benefit is that it has more flexibility and is less formal than the Corporation. It is important to note here that the key to these protections is they must be in the Company agreement to be sure that the maximum protections are in place. A poorly written company agreement - or worse, no Company agreement - can reduce the effectiveness of the LLC protection afforded by the charging order protection. Not all states provide the same level of charging order protections that states like Texas or Wyoming provide.

That flexibility presents itself at tax time. The LLC can be taxed in many different ways, depending if you qualify, based on the number of owners in the LLC. For example, if the LLC consists of just, you or you and your spouse, you have an opportunity to elect to be what is called a "disregarded entity." A disregarded entity is not required to file a tax return, the profits are reported on the owner's Form 1040 Tax Return. That is the default position, unless you elect otherwise. If you have two or more members, you can elect to be taxed as a Partnership, as a Corporation, or as an S-Corporation. As you can see, there are different opportunities available to maximize the flexible nature of the LLC business entity structure. Your homework will be to look at your personal tax situation with a tax professional to see how this type of tax election best fits in with your overall asset and income mix so that it can provide you with the best tax outcome. One mistake you do not want to make is deciding on anything purely based on the taxes. If you let the taxes determine what business you pursue or how you set things up, you are not necessarily going to have a profitable business. You want to set your business up in a profitable way while considering the best tax practices.

In Texas and a few other states, there is a variant of the LLC, called a Series LLC. This is essentially one LLC with several Series inside of it. Each series can have its own separate ownership, management, and assets. The liabilities of one Series are separate from those of another Series. This entity option is a fairly new concept as of the writing of this book (less than 10 years), so it does not have much case history. So, what does that mean to you? It means that the Series LLC has not been tested in the courts to identify the weaknesses. That being said, we are not recommending Series LLCs for all industries, especially not high-risk industries like trucking operations. The Series LLC is a good option to consider for real estate investing when multiple properties are involved.

Limited Partnership

There is one more business entity available in Texas, and in most states, that I would like to shed some light on. This option is more complicated, and I plan to cover it only briefly with you at this time without too much detail. If you would like to read more on this entity type, read my book, *The Road Map to Rich.* This business form is called the Limited Partnership. The Limited Partnership consists of at least two partners, a limited partner, and a general partner. You can have as many limited partners and as many general partners as you like. The general partner in this situation has full control of the business and calls all the shots, but at a price which is personal liability. When something goes wrong in a Limited Partnership, the general partner has personal liability for whatever happens, and they are NOT protected. Typically, the work around our firm will employ is to create the LLC to be the general partner that is owned by whoever the members or the managers are set to be. At that point, the LLC should work just like any other LLC as I have described before. The limited partners are then like the title implies, with limited liability, limited risk and they have limited voice and vote. Basically, the limited partners don't get much of a say unless the general partner is breaching their duties under the partnership agreement. It should be noted that, typically, it is difficult to establish that the general partner is breaching their duties because they have broad powers which they need to be able to manage the business and provide the necessary protection. There are a few other nuances and little wrinkles that are more complex, but in a nutshell, those are the different entity structures for business that we can implement in Texas. I explain this in more detail in my book, *The Road Map to Rich.*

For the Trucking industry, the Corporation, Limited Liability Company, and Limited Partnerships are good entities. But if we are starting from scratch (meaning we have not set up any entities yet) the ideal entity to use is the Limited Liability Company. It is important that the LLC be formed in a State that has favorable charging order protections. Another thing to consider is the privacy or anonymity of the owner of the Trucking Business and its related parts, which I will unpack later in the book.

A few states, including Wyoming, do not require the disclosure of the owners of the LLC, thereby making them anonymous as it relates to the ownership of the business. This can be helpful to keep out of the line of fire in a lawsuit.

Multiple entity structures are important to maximize the protections available. Your Wyoming LLC, if it is going to operate in Texas, will need to register with the Secretary of State for Texas, which will require the disclosure of the owners in order to grant authority to do business in Texas. The better way to preserve the anonymity is for the Wyoming LLC to own the Membership units of the Texas

LLC. This preserves the anonymous nature of the Wyoming LLC, while the Operations are done through the Texas LLC. Providing protection and privacy for the owners.

The Moving Parts Bucket

It is not enough to have great qualities; We should also have the management of them.

Francois De La Rochefoucauld

What exactly do we mean when we say moving parts? Moving parts include any kind of business operation in which you have employees, or own equipment that can hurt someone if misused, and has high customer interaction. To be clear, The Moving Parts Bucket is not an entity, but rather a category of entities. This Bucket will consist of as many entities as needed.

You will want one entity (LLC recommended) to have the MC and DOT Authority and other permissions to operate the Trucking Company. This also has the employees. You want another LLC to own your Trucks and another one to own your Trailers if applicable.

The Trucking Company owners know you can't control employees, including Drivers.

Employees (Drivers) are the ones who can cause damage they didn't intend to. It is easy to see how this can happen. Your driver is taking a load across the country, and a distracted driver cuts him off, and though your driver tries to avoid the collision, the accident happens. You know what is going to come next. Even when your driver is not at fault there can still be a lawsuit. Guess who has to respond?

The same can be said for the kind of businesses that have equipment or heavy machinery. Having trucks or trailers in your business, you want to make sure that you've got a separate entity for those types of business assets. You may even want to have a separate entity just to own that particular equipment and lease it to your separate operations company.

The best strategy is to separate what can be considered your high-risk operations of your operations. This would also include YOU, if you have an ongoing business or firm that depends on you for the bulk of the operations. Steps should be made to make sure you have a separate entity.

What exactly would separating yourself into an entity, as the main service provider, look like? There are options. You could be a corporation or an LLC; however, you do NOT want to be a sole proprietor, as I explained earlier and go into more detail in my book, *The Road Map To Rich.* In addition, you want to make sure that you separate the distinct types of risks. If you have a business that has heavy machinery and another business that is a restaurant, you want to separate the two within the Moving Parts Bucket. Tidiness is important when dealing with multiple businesses. Keeping these types of operations in the same entity will only create unnecessary connections, and if one of the entities suffers damage through a lawsuit or is attacked by some means, the other entity or entities will get wrapped in the mess. The basic rule of thumb is to create a separate entity for each business operation. To summarize, your operating entity should not own your trucks or trailers, and it definitely should not own your real estate. Which leads us to the next chapter, what is the Dirt Bucket.

The Dirt Bucket

"In the business world, the rearview mirror is always clearer than the windshield."

Warren Buffet, American Businessman

We may hate to think that our real estate triumphs have been fueled more by luck than a masterfully crafted study of the markets. Regardless of how you got to your own personal pot of real estate gold, you certainly need the right bucket to catch and care for that success; no matter how big or small your real estate portfolio may be. This leads our discussion to the second bucket of the 3 Bucket Method, the Dirt Bucket. Now as the name implies, this is where you want to keep your real estate.

I make it a personal rule not to put more than $500,000 dollars in aggregate value. That adds up to no more than $500,000 in total value of the properties. In other words, in a simple entity for example, if you have three rental houses that add up to $450,000, I'm okay with keeping those in a single LLC. If you own a million-dollar property. Well, you're not going to create two LLCs to own that property. It just doesn't make sense. You want to make sure you have just one entity for a property worth more than a million dollars or more than a half a million dollars or whatever you deem is your risk threshold.

In the Trucking Industry, the real estate component presents itself primarily in your warehouse, or terminal. This type of property can actually have a high dollar value. This property should be in a single purpose LLC. This LLC should only own this one property and nothing else. As your Trucking business grows, you may find greater opportunities for additional locations throughout the country to have other terminals. Each of those should be in a separate LLC.

One more thing that happens as you gain success with your Trucking Business, you fill find opportunities to invest in real estate outside of your own business industry. You may invest in a ranch, apartments, real estate developments, commercial property, or other types of real estate. All of the Dirt Bucket principles apply to any real estate investment. Properties should be kept separate if they are above your risk threshold.

Why even keep them separate? Wouldn't it be more expensive to set up and maintain? Let me tell you why it isn't. Imagine you own a $50,000 little rental house. You keep it in the same LLC as your terminal that's worth over two million dollars. If somebody gets hurt or killed on the little rental property, guess what? If they get a BIG judgment against your LLC as the owner, they're going to be able to get the terminal along WITH the little rental because they are owned by the same person or entity. It's important to keep those different properties separate.

Another important strategy is to separate your properties based on the quality of the risk. For instance, a commercial property has a certain quality of risk that is different from a residential or even ranch property.

Think about having a store front. During operating hours, you have the public coming in and out of your store front property and there are associated risks that can occur; someone might get hurt from those frequent contacts. Perhaps someone slips and falls in your store front. You may or may not be the owner of the property that makes up the store front. Maybe you are just renting the store front unit for your business. Whether you are renting to or renting from, you might be at risk; and both of you, the business owner, and the owner of the property, can be involved in a lawsuit. The owner of the property often-times is named as one of the defendants in a lawsuit. Certainly, something to keep in mind.

Allow me now to expand a bit on the different quality residential rentals. Albeit a different type of risk than commercial rental properties, residential rentals have their danger zones to be keenly aware of. This, of course, is where people will choose to live, not operate a business from; so, it may be safe to say they will take greater care of who comes in and out. With that said, you've got a little bit of risk mitigation built in. However, that does not negate the fact you still have somebody who is not you who will live in the rental, and therein lies the risk.

Literally. You've got stoves that, if left unattended, can start a fire. You've got a potential risk in slippery wet floors or bathtubs and other things in which people can get hurt. Your tenants have visitors. Your tenants have barbecues. Your tenants may use a pool you installed for the complex. A slew of different risks can be associated to living in any home or apartment rental, in general; the list goes on and on. And let us not forget the risks associated with owning raw land. Yes, they may be different in scale and quality, because with raw land, there are not as many people coming in, especially if you prepare the entrance of your land and other access points with “No Trespassing,” but ultimately somebody may come on to your property. It is important to remember you will be liable for certain unfortunate events that happen on your raw land, depending on your state's laws. Keep in mind, if somebody comes onto your land and there's an obvious danger and you haven't placed a warning sign in an obvious place, you could be liable for it because you knew, or should have known, about the danger.

One more risk to be aware of with property of any type is the “attractive nuisance.” This could be a swimming pool in the backyard, heavy machinery parked on a commercial property or even a pond on raw land. These things can attract people, especially children, who may not be able to discern the risk, and get hurt. You need to safeguard yourself from this risk.

Now that we have separated our risks, we can move onto the next bucket, The Paper Bucket.

The Paper Bucket: The Harmony Within

"Paper is poverty... it is only the ghost of money, and not money itself."

Thomas Jefferson, Founding Father

We want to fight to keep every asset we have and then sweat to multiply it. While sweating may not actually be a prerequisite to saving and multiplying your wealth, putting it in the next bucket, the Paper Bucket, is. In this bucket, we consolidate EVERYTHING. In this bucket, we would create a Limited Partnership or Limited Liability Company which would own your excess cash. The Paper Bucket would also own your stocks, bonds and other liquid assets that are not already protected by statute, either through the federal bankruptcy code or your state exemptions. Texas, where I mainly practice, is one of the states with the most favorable exemptions. So, in Texas, some things, like your retirement accounts and your personal residence, would not be something that you would want to put into your paper bucket, since they are already protected. Now, I know what you're thinking. I just finished explaining to separate everything from each other and now we're putting everything back together! You're right. The difference is the risk. To illustrate my point, let me tell you about two types of risk: internal risk and external risk.

The internal risk is the risk that comes from inside the business. Similar to the gears in a machine, in the Moving Parts Bucket, the risk comes primarily from these three things: the employees, the equipment and the things that the owner might do in the business contracts. An accident where one of your drivers hits someone while driving one of your trucks is an example of one of these items of risk in one single event. When it comes to business entities contained in the Dirt Bucket, the risk comes from the property itself. Any dangers, hazards, or the failure to maintain the actual property will present internal risks. A driver or vendor coming to your terminal steps into a pothole you have been meaning to fix, cracks their head open, and sues. That is the example of the Dirt Bucket internal risk.

Unlike the other two buckets, in the Paper Bucket, there is no internal risk because this bucket should only own paper assets such as cash, ownership interests, securities, bonds and things of that nature. Just owning shares in a company does not put personal liability on the owner. For example, if you own stock in Apple and Apple gets sued for something outrageous, you're not personally going to be worried about your assets other than a drop in the value of your stock in Apple. Apple stock value may go down; even to zero if Apple were to have a terrible loss. Hard to imagine, since Apple, as of the writing of this book, has been named the most profitable company in history. Either way, the rest of your personal assets would not be touched at all, and you would never worry about it, thanks to the way our laws are set up. Just being an owner of a company does not create personal liability.

External risk is the risk that comes from the outside. You must also consider the risk that comes from the owners. For instance, if you, as the owner of a company, get sued and your company is structured in a LLC, in Texas, the only thing a judgment creditor can do is get a charging order against your interest. The charging order directs the LLC to pay distributions to the person holding the charging order, whenever distributions are made. With the business entity structured as an LLC, you are not required to make distributions. Subsequently, the judgement creditor would not be able to manage or control your assets. They would just be stuck, holding the charging order papers, not able to do a thing. Meanwhile, you don't need to have the money in your hands. Your paper bucket entity can create another LLC to buy another real estate investment. You'll be ready for a fresh start with a new business from which you can be an employee and draw a salary from the new business.

As you can see, the Paper Bucket has an especially important role. Another name for the Paper Bucket entity is a Holding Company. As the name implies, this company will "hold" the shares of the other business operations. These three buckets are meant to work together as your business grows. This is where maintenance really becomes essential to the group.

The International Component

"Coming together is a beginning; keeping together is progress; working together is success."

Henry Ford, American Businessman

As a result of international treaties, there are many opportunities for trucking businesses from Canada, Mexico, and the United States to expand their trucking business. This chapter will discuss doing business in the United States by businesses and individuals from Mexico or Canada. To include both countries, without the need to keep repeating Canada and/or Mexico, I will simply refer to them as foreign.

Before we jump into doing business in the US, we need to talk about a type of tax that is not common in most countries, but is in the US, the United States Estate and Gift Tax. This is a transfer tax, not an income tax, so in theory you are not being taxed on your income twice. This tax as of the writing of this book is 40% of the value of the United States situs assets of a Non-Resident-Alien (NRA) to the United States. The tax used to be 55% when I started practicing law. There are certain items that are exempt from this tax, such as cash in bank accounts, and life insurance proceeds. Ownership interest in a business would be subject to the estate tax. Uncle Sam gives a credit before the tax takes effect. For US Citizens and Residents, this tax, as of the writing of this book, is over $12 million dollars of asset value before the tax is applicable. Unfortunately, Non-Resident-Aliens do not get the same treatment; the NRA estate tax credit is only $60,000. Therefore, it is particularly important to be cognizant of this tax exposure.

The most straight forward solution we recommend, and which works consistently, is to form a holding company in the foreign country to own the shares of the US Holding Company (Paper Bucket). With the ownership of the US assets completely in the name of a company, the estate tax will not be applicable to the asset. Since Canada and

Mexico do not have an estate tax, this tax is completely avoided. It is important to coordinate with your Accountant as the timing of the ownership can have other tax consequences that are beyond the scope of this book.

The structure would look like two layers in the Paper Bucket, followed by the ownership of the other assets through other Moving Parts or Dirt Bucket companies. When done properly, upon the death of an owner, there is no need for any probate administration in the US and no estate tax due in the US. Unfortunately, sometimes people delay decisions and don't get to things in time.

We recently had a client who was already doing business in the US, and we recommended a restructuring plan for better protection from a direct liability point of view and an estate tax exposure point of view. They wanted to think about what the changes would mean for their business in Mexico. Unfortunately, the patriarch who was the primary owner of the business, including the US business shares, died before they could make a decision. As a result, their successful business has taken a big hit; 40% of the value of the business is going to have to be paid to the IRS. This will hamper their plans to grow since a large chunk of capital is being taxed. Taking action promptly is important in order to take full advantage of the opportunities that the law provides for us.

If they had implemented our proven system, there would not have been any estate tax due, and the operations could have continued uninterrupted. Addressing the estate tax liability exposure is a key consideration when you are a Non-Resident-Alien.

It could cost your family 40% of your business.

Maintenance Of Your System

"The best way to predict the future is to create it."

Peter Drucker, Austrian-American Author

As an owner of a Trucking Business, you can appreciate the need for maintenance of your equipment. For example, if you have a brand-new truck and you put it to work, it will operate well and generate money for you. Now imagine if for this same truck, you never change the oil, check the tire pressure, add DEF or windshield washer fluid, or even wash it. At some point it will become a brick in your yard that not only does not produce for you, but one that actually becomes a risk for you.

With that in mind, it is important to properly maintain your business entities, especially once you have two or more entities. I know you can appreciate the importance of maintenance from the perspective of the Trucking Business. So, how does maintenance work for entities? What happens at the "shop" when you take your entities in for maintenance?

The 3 Bucket Method includes maintaining each entity in each bucket and ensuring the integrity of the protections that have been put in place. There are some key items that we need to make sure are covered each year to insure we are in compliance and well protected. The following is the process we use for our 3 Bucket Method Risk Audit:

Minutes

Minutes are the only way that a business entity "speaks." When there is a resolution, minutes document what the company decided to do during a given period of time. Minutes becomes a record of the actions approved by the company and its management. When was the last time your company had minutes and recorded the decisions the company made? This sometimes can be a tricky thing to keep up with. As business owners, we are busy running our business. The transportation business is on 24-7, so it is not always convenient to have meetings and document decisions taken. But, when there is no record, others (like the IRS or plaintiff's attorneys) can put "words in the entity's mouth." This is why having regular minutes, whether they are required by law or not, is important to have in place.

Leases

As you start to fill in your buckets and add real estate, you will likely be your own tenant. This is a time where it is critical to have contracts between the companies. This contract documents what the rent amount will be and what the terms are related to it. Failing to have a clear separation of the entities with a contract can cause them to collapse and expose the asset we were trying to protect.

Would you let someone move into your property and start operating their business, or would you let someone move into your house and start living there, without some contract in writing including rent that would be charged and rules of responsibilities? Probably not, at least not for anyone that is not related to you. The same thing is important to realize about the actual payment of rent. The rent payment needs to be made to the Landlord, not to the Landlord's bank.

I can't stress enough the importance of having lease agreements in place that have been approved by both entities' minutes. This documents the separateness of the companies and reinforces the fact that two different companies are entering into an agreement at arm's length.

Equipment Leases

The Trucking industry is very capital-intensive. What I mean by this is that you need a lot of assets, in this case trucks and trailers, in order to produce a healthy profit in the trucking business. Implementing the 3 Bucket Method, we separate the ownership of the equipment from the ownership of the operations. The relationship between these businesses requires formal documentation of the responsibilities of each party. This is of key importance for you. It is important to document who has the responsibility to screen and select the drivers of the trucks and who is responsible for the maintenance of the equipment. These are the two points that are brought up to place liability on the Trucking company. In the equipment lease we document that, as part of the agreement to have access to the equipment, the Lessee is responsible for selecting the driver of the equipment and everything that that entails. Additionally, the Lessee is responsible for conducting all maintenance on the equipment. It is important to remember that this contract will not be enforceable against the plaintiff in a lawsuit, but rather it will be evidence that shows that the responsibility for the maintenance and driver selection was squarely on one of the parties, and that the other party was not responsible for these items.

It is important to have these agreements up to date with the trucks and trailers in the fleet, to add new acquisitions and remove sold or traded equipment. As with all of these agreements it is important for these to be confirmed and documented in the entity minutes for both the Lessor and the Lessee.

Loans/Promissory Notes

Financing is a key part of any business. This can be from third party financing, such as banks, and finance companies when we are purchasing property and equipment. Additionally, working capital is critical in the Trucking industry, and factoring can be an important source of cash flow. At times there will be cash available in one company, but it is needed to pay a debt in another. This is when an inter-company loan may be made, either by paying the debt directly to the lender on behalf of the other company or transferring funds to the company so it can pay it from its own account.

All of these loans should be documented using a promissory note to evidence the transaction. It should also be recorded in the minutes of the companies, both lender and borrower. This may seem to be a bit overkill for just a simple loan to cover a payment between companies with common ownership. The following analogy will explain the importance of this documentation.

Often when I speak on the 3 Bucket Method, I will ask the audience, "Who will lend me $10,000.00 without signing something saying I will pay you back?" I think you can guess how many hands go up. That's right, ZERO. Why, as much as they may like me, and trust me, they would like some documentation that I agree to pay this debt back and something they can use to compel me. When one of your companies lends money to another, and there is no documentation, it is as if they moved money from one pocket to another, which unfortunately may be what the owners feel it is. The stakes are too high for this attitude. The plaintiff's attorney in a lawsuit will use the above analogy against you and say to the jury "If they don't respect the separateness of the companies, Jury, neither should you." They will suggest that the companies are not two separate companies, but one company with the assets of both companies available to settle the judgement.

You can see documentation is extremely important, especially when you are dealing with money, for any of your businesses. Do not let this step get skipped; it will come back and bite you, at the most inconvenient time. Think during a lawsuit or a tax audit, either federal (IRS) or state. Be sure to document these transactions.

The Rest Of Your Tool Kit

"There's no harm in hoping for the best as long as you've prepared for the worst."

Stephen King, author

What else should be in your 3 Bucket Method "tool kit"? Insurance and a good Estate Plan are two critical pieces that should be in your tool kit.

Insurance

It can be critical that you make sure you have personal and business liability insurance, not to mention the correct amount of insurance for your business. For the trucking industry there are specific insurance requirements just to be able to operate. There are two reasons you want to have the proper amount of insurance. Number one, you want to make sure that you are a good business citizen and are ready to make things right when things at your business go wrong. Ask yourself, are you prepared with the right tools to take care of your customers if your employees do something that hurts a customer and puts your business in jeopardy? There is insurance for that, and you want to be sure you have that set up.

Secondly, you want to make sure that somebody is going to pay for the attorneys you will need to hire to defend you if there's a loss. It's not cheap. If you're footing the bill, you could easily spend $100,000 in legal fees to defend your case right up to the date of trial. It can be extremely expensive. Make it a point to make sure you've got the liability insurance you need by checking in with an expert.

Other insurance that is important for Trucking is vehicle liability and non-owned vehicle liability. This is important when your employees are driving their own vehicles for your business or as part of their job. Worker's Compensation insurance can likewise provide peace of mind in the event of an employee injury. Some states require this insurance, while other states create substantial disincentives for not having it. In Texas, you waive many defenses if you do not have worker's compensation insurance.

Key Man life insurance is another insurance that you might not otherwise consider part of asset protection. Let me explain. Key Man life insurance is a life insurance policy on a key employee (which could be you, the owner). The purpose of this insurance is to provide funds to the company to pay to hire someone to do the deceased employee duties. Having the liquidity to hire a new CEO after the previous one passes unexpectedly can help save the business from quickly withering away.

There are other types of insurance that you want to review with your Insurance agent, like cyber protection, errors and omissions, terrorism, etc. Work with your insurance agent to be sure that you are properly protected.

As you can see, identifying and separating your risk into different buckets as described in my 3 Bucket Method provides you, as the business owner, protection from both sides of the risk equation. By employing the 3 Bucket Method to enjoy the benefits of asset protection planning, you are smartly mitigating the vast majority of the internal and external challenges that face your important assets. And why do we do any of this? To prepare a path towards *generational wealth*. Unlike wealth that we only enjoy in our lifetimes, generational wealth is wealth to be enjoyed and protected for our children, our children's children and, God willing, the generations that follow. This leads to the discussion of the benefits of estate planning.

Estate Planning For Generational Wealth

Another often overlooked part of your toolkit includes having an estate plan. Without a good plan, your family could be exposed to Estate taxes, and attorney fees that could have been eliminated or reduced.

Some states have an overly complicated and expensive probate system and as a result, it can be very costly to go to probate. In Texas, we have an efficient system, IF you have a Will. It is possible to take advantage of some potentially expeditious estate planning strategies, but you need to make sure that you've got some sort of plan. That said, a

Will means you will have to do some sort of Probate to effectuate the will.

If you don't have a Will, even in Texas, it can get expensive to probate an estate. Saying that, the next thing you want to do is make sure you have an estate plan in place. That basically comes down to having your Will in order and, in many cases, having your trust in place. You need the right instruments to make a smooth transition to the next generation. One of the most important things you can do in your lifetime is know who you are leaving your assets to before you die and ensure that they are able to receive those assets in an efficient manner. Remember, a Will does not avoid probate. A Will is not effective until a Judge admits the will to Probate, meaning that we have to go to court in order to give it power and authority.

A Living Trust/Revocable Trust may be a key component. This would allow you to avoid probate and the court process to reduce the time and expense of transferring your assets to your family. Additionally, the Revocable Trust can reduce the risk of litigation because it will typically have a longer track record and is more difficult to challenge than a Will. In order to attach the Revocable Trust, a party will have to file an original lawsuit, not just join the existing probate as when using a Will in your estate plan.

The way the Revocable Trust works is that it is an agreement between three parties. The first party is the Settlor, the person who creates the trust and initially funds it. The second party is the Trustee, the person who manages the trust and makes the decisions regarding the trust within the limits of the Trust agreement. The last party is the Beneficiary, the person for whom all of this is being done. Using the Revocable Trust plan, you would play all three roles while you are alive and have capacity. Once you pass, your successor trustee simply takes the trust assets and distributes them based on the directions outlined in the Trust agreement, without the need to go to court for probate.

When we prepare Revocable Trusts, we also prepare a Will, which we call a "Pour Over Will." This type of Will transfers your Probate assets that were not titled in the name of the trust to the Revocable trust for the distribution pursuant to the Trust.

Some other documents, or “tools,” to have in mind are a Durable Power of Attorney; Medical Power of Attorney; Directive to Physicians, Family and Surrogates; and Designation of Guardians. I refer to these as powers and directives.

The Durable Power of Attorney (POA) grants your agent authority to make fiscal related decisions. This can be written in a way that it is only activated when you are incapacitated as determined by your physician. This is important to authorize your agent to deal with others in the event of your incapacity. It is also important to know that upon death the POA no longer has effect. Likewise, in the event a Guardianship is placed on you, the POA is dissolved.

The Medical Power of Attorney (MPOA) grants your agent authority to make medical or health care decisions on your behalf in the event that you are incapacitated, again as determined by your physician. This also allows your agent to discuss your healthcare with your physician. You can include special instructions in your MPOA; I had a client request that they continue to receive acupuncture treatments by a person certified in a particular school of acupuncture. Like the POA, the MPOA dissolves in the event a guardianship is placed on you, and it terminates upon your death.

The Directive to Physicians, Family and Surrogates, allows you to direct actions in the event of two scenarios. If you are suffering from a terminal condition in which you have less than 6 months to live, or if you are suffering from an irreversible condition in which you cannot care for yourself or make decisions for yourself and will die without continued life sustaining treatment. You will have two choices to select from for each of these scenarios. The first option is to remove all life-sustaining treatments other than those to keep you comfortable and let you die as gently as possible. The second option is to maintain you in this condition using the available life-sustaining treatment. There is no wrong answer; it is only your choice. Then the importance of this document is that it informs your family of your wishes, and it takes the burden of making this choice off of your family's shoulders.

The Designation of Guardians comes in two varieties. The first is the selection of a guardian for you in the event of future incapacity. This allows you to select who a court should appoint as your guardian in the event that you are determined to be suffering from an incapacity. You can also select who you do not want to serve as your guardian. There are two guardian types. The guardian of the person makes decisions and is responsible for your physical wellbeing, such as eating, bathing, taking medications, etc. The other type of guardian is the guardian of the estate. The guardian of the estate is responsible for and makes decisions regarding your fiscal assets. Both of these can be the same person or different persons, and both are under the supervision of the court.

SECTION TWO

Moving Parts Bucket in the Real World

Okay, so now you have your business set up in the right business entity structure. Again, not a partnership and not a sole proprietorship, but rather in one of these three entities: an LLC or Limited Liability Company, my preferred type; a Corporation, my second preferred; and finally, a Limited Partnership, which can be employed in the right circumstances. In an operating or "the moving parts bucket", we are looking at implementing the LLC more than anything else. Now we ask, what are you going to put in your LLC? Let me give you an example to understand what would be best.

I have many clients in the trucking business. We have set up many 3 Bucket Method Structures for this industry. Here we will go over the different moving parts bucket entities and what their roles are for the trucking business.

The first entity in the moving parts business is the entity that has the Motor Carrier authority or MC number. The trucking operation basically hires truck drivers and has trucks (but does not own the trucks or the trailers); these trucks travel throughout the United States delivering merchandise to warehouses as directed under the bill of lading for your customers. Let's unpack that scenario. The business owners have business assets and equipment, such as 18-wheelers, tractors, and trailers: heavy-duty machines that can cause a lot of damage. Truck drivers are human beings and can have accidents or make unintended mistakes that have consequences. Operation owners also have customers whose merchandise they are transporting that can be damaged if there is an accident on the highways. How do we mitigate those types of risks in the moving parts bucket for this particular line of business? The Moving Parts Structure for this client involves creating an LLC to be the trucking business, which is to have the MC Authority or Permits to conduct the business. As a result, the trucking company LLC gets hired to move freight throughout the country. We then set up another LLC to own the trucks that make up the equipment. As you may know, these trucks are expensive pieces of equipment. Purchased new, these trucks can be well over a hundred thousand dollars each. Our technique is to separate the equipment from the business operation by protecting it in a separate LLC. We will call it the Equipment LLC. Why, you ask? Well, if there is a lawsuit against the Trucking LLC because an employee of the trucking company was in an accident, only one truck might be lost because it is damaged and out of commission, and not the whole fleet. Let me explain further. The fleet of trucks and trailers is owned by the Equipment LLC. The Equipment LLC leases the trucks and trailers to the Trucking LLC; however, that contract specifies that the Trucking LLC has the responsibility for maintenance of the trucks and the responsibility for assuring that the drivers are safe and qualified. Any consequences from the misuse or damages are the Trucking LLC's only.

If someone sues the LLC that hired the driver that had the accident, they can only get the desks, computers, and other miscellaneous stuff they have since that company does not essentially own the trucks. Basically, they can't take away what isn't "owned", since the Trucking LLC is just leasing the trucks from the Equipment LLC that was created. To reiterate, if you have the ownership of the equipment outside of the Trucking LLC, in that lawsuit, the only truck that is getting lost is the one that was in the accident because of the damage sustained. So, we're able to push all the liability onto the Trucking LLC. As you can see, in the Trucking LLC we have all the risk and we have as few assets as necessary. Be sure to have enough assets to properly and financially operate (low value assets) or lease (high value assets). In our recommended structuring we usually form three LLCs in the moving parts bucket: the equipment LLC (for the trucks that are leased to the trucking LLC), one for trailers (yes, the trailer LLC) that carry the merchandise, and one for the trucking LLC (the primary business).

As you can see, we create different entities in the moving parts bucket. One of the benefits in regard to taxes is that lease income is not subject to employment taxes, as of the writing of this book. As a result, you save about 15 percent when you are both the employer and the employee. This allows you to move income and create income that has a lower tax liability. And all of this is perfectly legal as long as you are doing it within the acceptable ranges of the rent that you are charging; you can't charge a ridiculously high rent that doesn't make any sense for what you are doing. It has to have a business purpose and has to make business sense when you are doing this. I hope this helps you understand the different things you want to put in the moving parts bucket.

I will share a story of a trucking client of mine, who before he met me had all of his trucks, trailers, and equipment in his trucking company with MC Authority. His driver was in an accident and a lawsuit resulted. For some reason, the insurance company failed to show up at the trial of the case and the court rendered a judgement in the amount of $4,000,000 against my client. This is about the time he came to me. Fortunately for him, the opposing attorney saw the insurance company's failure as a bigger opportunity for him, and they entered an agreement in which the rights to pursue the insurance company were assigned to the plaintiff (who had won the case), and my client's company was absolved of further liability. I asked my client how he thought he could pay this or if the company had sufficient assets to pay this judgement. He let me know that if it had not been for this 12th hour settlement, this accident would have put him out of business. We have since implemented the 3 Bucket Method in his business, and he is in a much better position in the event of another accident (even another judgement).

The Dirt Bucket In The Real World

Now let's explore the Dirt bucket. In the dirt bucket, you want to put your real estate investments. You will want to separate it based on risk. The key thing is to determine your personal risk tolerance level. For me, it's $500,000. For you, it might be $750,000 or $250,000. Or perhaps it’s a single asset that is in excess of your risk limit. In this case, the best strategy is to use a single LLC.

Banks like it when you have a single entity for your assets. So, if you've got a million-dollar property the banks are going to be incredibly happy that you do not just have it in YOUR name, but rather, in an LLC all by itself. Why? Well, number one, banks hate to deal with anyone who is not their customer. With that said, if you use an LLC dirt bucket for your real estate investments, they won't have to worry about you doing something that creates a liability (for example, getting sued and then consequently having to deal with someone else trying to take away that particular asset or any associated equity from you). Reason number two is, if you have your real estate in an LLC in which the property is the only asset and they are the only lender, then they're not worried about anything else going on in your life. They can focus their attention on other things, knowing this real estate asset is isolated in an LLC. The main concern, in their eyes, is if you are paying your note on time. The caveat to that is residential mortgage-lending companies are not going to be able to lend you money in the name of your LLC. If you move a home to an LLC or are seeking a home mortgage, lenders will not be able to provide the loan to an LLC for real estate. This and other issues may arise that you need to be aware of when creating these business entity structures. Keep in mind there is not a 100% way of mitigating all risk, and situations need to be evaluated on an individual basis. I would be happy to discuss your particular situation in an attorney/client privilege conversation.

Now we know that we want to have a separate dirt bucket for our real estate or "dirt" so to speak, but how does that work? Let’s unpack this and see how this bucket plugs into the overall system. But before we get to that stage, let's talk about the different types of real estate that can come into play. Imagine you are interested in beginning your journey as a real estate investor. Typically, the first way a lot of people start on this real estate path is by buying a residential property and renting it. It might be a small house, a condominium or maybe a small apartment complex. There can be a lot of available inventory coupled with a high need for affordable housing in your area, which makes this type of investment appealing. You may even consider renting out the house you used to live in and have moved on from when you outgrew it. I won't be able to cover every single type of real estate, because one property type is almost as different as the other, but I'm going to cover some general concepts to keep in mind. You can learn more about different types of real estate and real estate strategies in my book The Road Map to Rich.

Commercial property is our next concept to digest and, in and of itself, is pretty broad. Commercial property can include some residential type properties, like a big apartment building. It can include a business center or a shopping strip center. It can be one unit in a shopping center, or it might be structured as a condominium in which there is common ownership of the parking lot and buildings. However, inside each unit there are individual owners.

Raw land is another type of investment. You can have a ranch that you use for hunting, grazing, ranching, or farming. That raw land has a value. It may or may not always be income-producing; it may just be a little something that you invested in for the future. It could be a property you bought that is undeveloped, and you're just waiting for the growth of the city or county to reach your property so you can enjoy the increase in value in that part of the town or city. You may be in a situation where you're not going to be generating a lot of income from your raw land investment. If you have the cash flow and the ability to pay the taxes and maintain that property, then that's a whole other discussion. Let’s say that land is the investment you've chosen; having it in an LLC works really well. Your administrative costs will be relatively low because your real estate is not going to require many transactions. You're basically going to be paying one check for taxes and one check for your insurance if you've already bought the property free and clear. Those are the three general types of real estate properties that are out there.

Let me tell you about another client, who has around two million dollars in rental properties in South Texas. He has a higher risk tolerance than me. His property is located in two regions, and he decided to separate his risk along those lines. We created two entities, one to own his northern properties and another to own his southern properties. This client has separated his risk and will not lose everything in the event of a lawsuit.

Remember, each of these has different associated risks. If you have multiple properties that are valued at less than half a million dollars, such as in the example I mentioned earlier, you could bring all the properties together. As I mentioned before, sometimes your properties are from different risk pools. In other words, some might be commercial, some might be residential, some might be raw land, and maybe they don't all add up to $500,000. You will still want to consider separating them by their different risk qualities.

Let me address the most common property purchased in this structure for a trucking business: a terminal or warehouse. This type of property is ideal for using a single purpose LLC. This LLC will then rent the property to the trucking LLC. Using market-based rent, you can move income to the real estate LLC while creating an expense for the Trucking LLC. You should discuss this strategy with your CPA or tax advisor to see what an acceptable range is and what will provide the most benefit to you. In the event of any lawsuit against the Trucking LLC, the property is completely separated from this; and to the extent necessary, Real Estate LLC can terminate the lease and lease the property to another company, even another owned by the same person or group.

In the situation where you own multiple properties, it may be useful to create a series LLC in which each Property is owned by a series which makes up the LLC. In essence, each series is separate from the other series and their owners. The liabilities of one series cannot be imputed to another series. This provides good asset protection in that each series can be owned in the LLC but has individual protection. The series can be self-contained with maximum protection and minimal formation cost. It is definitely worth considering the

Series LLC if you have multiple real estate properties.

The Paper Bucket In The Real World

"Take care of your body. It's the only place you have to live."

Jim Rohn, American Entrepreneur

If you do a fantastic job managing your money, you will experience a great return on your investment; and I can help you create and use the right tools to do so. In the Paper Bucket, you will have an opportunity to do some estate planning that will allow for additional asset protection. This is a place where you might consider doing a Limited Partnership. I know I said before that there are few situations where I recommend a Limited Partnership entity. This is one of those. Before we move forward with that concept, let me first say, as I explained previously, your Paper Bucket is where you want to have all your liquid assets. This will include your paper assets, your membership certificates in your other companies, and your excess cash from your business. This would be the time to pull out that excess cash and be sure it's not sitting in your personal bank account. Likewise, you will want to sweep your business accounts to pull out excess cash beyond what is needed to properly capitalize your various companies. Additionally, make sure that you also have your ownership in stocks and anything that's not already protected by statute in your Paper Bucket entity. Of the three buckets, this is the only bucket that typically has only one company. That can change if you are a married couple, and you have separate property that is in different buckets or has different ownership interests. I don’t plan to get into much detail about family situations, but I can discuss these with you in person. It’s just outside the scope and detail of this book.

Again, in your Paper Bucket, you're going to go ahead and have either an LLC or a Limited Partnership with the purpose of holding your shares in your other businesses, your cash, etc. Using this method has helped many of my clients, especially those who are in partnerships with other people. The Limited Partnership or the LLC is the preferred entity that my clients use to invest for a few reasons. If there's a disagreement in what the distributions are going to be, especially if one of the partners in the deal gets a charging order, the investment in the new venture is done by the paper bucket LLC, not the individual, thereby further protecting and insulating my clients. Basically, if there's a charging order or if there is a problem personally with the other partner, it's not going to affect their investment in that other company. The charging order will go to an actual person who owns The Paper Bucket. Another reason my clients use a Limited Partnership for the Paper Bucket is because this is where we've consolidated all of their assets within the business structure, and it becomes owned centrally by this company. Another way to look at it is that the Paper Bucket becomes their personal mutual fund. The personal mutual fund is going to be what my clients can leave to their heirs, to their chosen charity, or WHATEVER they want to do with their assets. It provides part of their estate plan. They can give part of it in life to have their heirs learn to manage the wealth they will eventually receive.

Essentially, the paper bucket LLC is the main asset that you will own directly. It is the only thing that can be attacked in the event of a personal judgement or personal lawsuit. They will only be able to get a charging order against the shares of the LLC, but they will not be able to control or force the liquidation of the LLC assets. As a result, the assets owned are protected from these external forces.

I will add one more wrinkle as I have many international clients. When you have Non-United States Citizens or Non-Residents, it is important to consider forming a foreign company to serve as an additional paper bucket company. The foreign company should own the US paper bucket company. There is a good reason for recommending this: in the United States, we have something called the Estate and Gift Tax. This tax is currently charged at a rate of 40% of the value of the estate. As of writing this, for US Citizens this tax starts on every dollar after $12,060,000; however, non-resident aliens pay the tax on their US assets (which includes the US companies) after $60,000. So, for many trucking companies owned by non-resident aliens, upon their deaths, there will be a high tax to pay. If the shares of the US company are owned by a foreign company, then the estate tax does not apply to those interests, as I stated earlier in this book.

THE COLLABORATIVE EFFORT

"Alone, we can do so little; together, we can do so much." –

Helen Keller, American Author

For most businesspeople who are just starting out, it's safe to say they don't have all three buckets in place. They may not need all three; or perhaps their business has not yet matured enough, and they are just not there yet. That's okay. And although each of the three buckets can be implemented on their own, collaboration, like carbonation, certainly mixes things up in an effective way. By putting the Moving Parts Bucket and Dirt Bucket together to work side by side for your business, you will experience a tangible maturation of your business. You will feel the "next level" approaching. How will you know when to take your business to the next level? Maybe you started out by renting a terminal or warehouse. Your business has grown and needs more space, and maybe you made some money and are now tired of paying rent. Now do you buy or rent? Rent and ownership of your business space should be considered carefully and are each a whole separate ball of wax. In some cases, renting is the smartest thing to do; in other cases, ownership is the smartest thing to do. You may want to own the property even though, in the big scheme of things, you may be better off just renting. But for our example, let's say your business is growing and you need more space. You have decided to stop renting and own your own space. That will allow for more control over your environment. There is also what I call the "third case," where sometimes you just need to do what you WANT to do. You will usually know best how to handle each situation, and the reality is, what you really want to do is what will result; and oftentimes we learn a whole lot more in "the third case." The key in the third case is that you are aware of the pros and cons of the options, but you decide with maximum knowledge.

Back to my example, and how you implement the Moving Parts and the Dirt Bucket to work together. By owning your own space for your business, you have now transitioned to a two-bucket operation with the addition of the Dirt Bucket to your Moving Parts Bucket. How did that happen? Simple. You used the Dirt Bucket in the form of an LLC to buy that new terminal. Pretty easy, right? It’s important to have the ownership of your terminal owned by a separate company, and I prefer an LLC. I typically don't recommend Corporations for real estate businesses. Corporations create a lot of tax liabilities that, under current law, will hit the moment you want to sell the property. With the Dirt Bucket now in place, the Dirt Bucket entity that owns the terminal then rents it to your Moving Parts Bucket entity. You have to make sure that you have extremely specific lease agreements in place to ensure the success of employing these two buckets together. The lease agreements must have clear explanations as to who has responsibility for what. It is critical that your Moving Parts entity is the one that has the majority of the risks and is the one that then has the responsibilities. Why? Because it doesn't own any assets and truly has little to lose.

This is the ideal way to structure your business and will result in a lease agreement between your operations company, the Moving Parts Bucket, and your real estate company, the Dirt Bucket. Before you finish checking off your to-do list as complete, the next step is to make sure that you have insurance in place to cover the general liability property in the event there is ever a lawsuit and if you need the ability to terminate the contract. Additionally, you want to have insurance to pay for the attorneys to represent the owner of the property, as well as separate attorneys to represent the business owner that operates in that location.

To give you a real world visual, some of our clients who have put this strategy into practice have the operations of the business, equipment leasing, and real estate ownership in their terminal each in their own entity. They charge rent to their equipment leasing company. That becomes an expense to the operations company that is deductible, which then becomes income to the real estate company in order to make enough money to cover the note, pay the property taxes and any other expenses that the real estate company is going to be responsible for. Essentially, that is how those two buckets connect and minimize your risk as a business owner.

Gifting Assets

"I have found that among its other benefits, giving liberates the soul of the giver." –

Maya Angelou, American Poet

It's always nice to receive, but in the business world, it can be nicer, or at least more strategic, to give. So, let's discuss gifting your assets. As of the writing of this book, the estate tax credit is right around 12.06 million per person. For married couples, we are talking about 24+ million dollars' worth of assets. This is the total amount a person can leave to their heirs without being subject to the estate tax, which, as of the writing of this book, is 40%. Anything over this is subject to estate tax. With that said, not a lot of people are going to be too worried about the estate tax. However, there is a gift tax which uses up those applicable exclusion amounts, the credit we discussed above. If you are strategic, you can transfer your money without paying the estate and gift tax. How exactly does that work? Perhaps you want to gift part of your company, but you don't want to let go of the control.

You can make a gift of a Limited Partnership Interest, continue being a general partner through an LLC, and continue being a limited partner. When you make distributions and you want to give distributions to your kids, they would get distributions based on their percentage ownership in the partnership. This is another example of using a Limited Partnership as the type of business entity for gifting. If, on the other hand, you decide to use an LLC for gifting instead, that's when you have majority rules and you need to make sure you keep a majority interest to keep the control.

But before you make your gifts, you've got to look at the equation carefully. Will it be worth gifting property if you create a capital gains bill for your kids? You don't want to shoot yourself in the foot with your generosity. Let's say your assets are worth a million dollars and you want to give your kids a million dollars. The million dollars comes in the form of a real estate asset, like a warehouse or terminal that you inherited from a relative that died 40 years ago. The basis, or cost of the property, was received at the date of death of your last relative who owned and left it to you. And let's say that the basis is $300,000, but it's worth a million dollars today. If you sell it today, you're going to have a capital gains tax based on the difference of $700,000 that you could be taxed on; assuming the capital gains rate at 20%, the tax bill will be $140,000. Alternatively, if you gift it to your kids, they will receive it with the tax basis of $300,000. If they decide to sell it, they're going to pay the capital gains tax based on the $700,000 profit. If your kids inherit it there will be an adjustment in the basis on the date of your death. When that adjustment happens, it's called a "step up in basis." As a result, since you have to pay tax on the value at the date of death, the IRS lets you increase your basis to the fair market value at the date of death.

So, the basis that your kids inherited at is going to be a million dollars; and if they sell it for that same million dollars, no capital gains tax would be due at that time. At that time, you will need to decide whether you want to do any gifting or not; you have some options. Using a Limited Partnership, you can transfer up to 99% without losing control. Using an LLC, you are limited and can't gift more than 51%. Once you go past 51%, you lose the ability to have full control of the entity. For some things you may need 70% of the vote. With that being said, you want to be sure you carefully draft your company agreement before you start making gifts. Another element for discussion of the Paper Bucket is “who owns the Paper Bucket?” Another layer of privacy can be created when creating trust, and this strategy typically works best when we create everything upfront. For some clients, we've created trusts, and the trust owns the Paper Bucket. The trust becomes an instrument and does not need to be filed anywhere. A trust would also say and control who will get your shares in the partnership or LLC when you pass away. When discretion and privacy are priorities, using a trust could wind up being the dead end for somebody trying to poke around and find out who owns what. The individual person’s name of the beneficiary never appears anywhere. If you don't have a trust, you should at least have a Will. Let me take a moment to take my estate planner hat off and speak to you as your good friend because I can’t say it enough: EVERYBODY needs to have a Will. If you own anything, including a business or if you have kids, you need to have a Will. It is that simple. Having versus not having a Will can be like night and day. With a Will in place, you can say how things are to be distributed upon your death, which allows for instruction and a smooth transition for your family. Not having a Will can create a firestorm of uncertainty, as well as a financial burden due to infighting between family members; this ultimately causes all kinds of problems that could have easily been avoided. Sometimes equal and fair are not the same thing.

A Trust is another way to distribute your estate. The difference is that you transfer your estate to the trust and when you die it passes based on the Trust without court involvement. In many states, including Texas, this is the best way to go. Now, it's better to have something rather than nothing. I've seen the popular online-generated Wills get admitted into probate and work; but they created a lot of problems for the family because the online-generated Will didn't include certain language that allowed for independent administration, which makes probate easier in Texas. The online-generated Will sometimes didn't distribute the assets in a way that was based on the heirs involved in the family business. For the majority of my clients, just writing a Will on a computer does not address a slew of issues that need to be considered. Think about your hairstyle for a moment. Sure, you can cut your own hair, but why would you when you can have your hair cut by a studied professional who can see and style your hair from all angles, giving you the best result? Some things are best left to the help of a professional who has expertise in dealing with your situation so that you're able to make the best plan for you. You don't just wake up and say, "I'm going to write my entire Will right after I drink my cup of coffee." Consider the bigger picture and make a plan, your Estate Plan. And no matter the size of your estate, plan on how things are to be distributed upon your death, because the reality is death is the end of the road for all of us at some point.

Not Quite Dead Yet

"Lancelot:	*Brave, brave Concorde! You shall not have died in vain!*
Concorde:	*Uh, I'm-I'm not quite dead, sir.*
Lancelot:	*Well, you shall not have been mortally wounded in vain!*
Concorde:	*Uh, I-I think uh, I could pull through, sir.*
Lancelot:	*Oh, I see."*

Monty Python and the Holy Grail

Another possible reality is that you might not die per se. You might become incapacitated, perhaps as a result of a stroke or car accident. You may be in a situation where you become permanently or temporarily disabled and can't take care of yourself. Even in times like these, you may be in a situation where you need to take a business action and you can't. What in the world can you do then? In the real world, unfortunate things like this happen all the time. But you don't have to feel helpless because there are tools you can put in place that will offer you and your family security. Let me provide an example. Let's say you found a piece of raw land with plenty of potential. You then put a contract on this piece of raw land for $100,000 and soon after suffer a car accident that puts you in a coma that you will recover from, but not until after four months. You're not able to make decisions or sign any closing documents during that time. In the meantime, while you were sleeping in your coma, Wal-Mart announces that they are going to set up their new Supercenter right next door to your contracted property, bringing its worth from $100,000 to one million dollars. Your seller is highly likely going to try to get out of the deal. They're going to say, since you can't sign the closing, they will want to cancel the contract and let the time expire; and then you end up losing your opportunity. They, in turn, will try to sell it to somebody else for a million dollars. Instead of you making the money and your family benefiting, it's going to be this other person. So how do you protect yourself? You need the right documents with the power to protect you. With a Durable Power of Attorney, you can make sure that whoever you decide is the Power of Attorney can sign those closing documents for that property for $100,000 on your behalf. You will then own the property, turn around, and sell it for the million dollars, and you and your family can benefit from that lucrative deal, as opposed to the seller who wanted to back out. I hope that sends home the importance of these powers of attorney.

Next to consider is having a Medical Power of Attorney. A Medical Power of Attorney is somebody you have chosen to make health care decisions. This person can be the same person as your Durable Power of Attorney or a different person.

It is also important to consider who will be your designated guardian. A designated guardian is somebody you have chosen to take care of you if there is a court proceeding that needs to happen due to your illness or otherwise. It is better to select the best person to represent you in court ahead of time and not rely on the court's good judgment. There have been plenty of occasions when no one has been selected, and someone without the best intentions presents themselves in front of the court and says, "Hey, I want to be the guardian;" and just like that, it's done.

One of the greatest benefits to having these documents in place is removing the burden from your family to make these tough decisions at the end of life. There is a document we can create called Directive to Physicians, Family and Surrogates where you can indicate what you want to happen if you're in a terminal condition or in an irreversible condition. Do you want them to just pull the plug and let you die as gently as possible, or do you want them to do everything they can to keep you alive? You have the power to choose, and with the proper documents in place, you will have the security that what you want to happen will happen.

A Trust can also be invaluable in the management of your assets while you are incapacitated. The Trustee will manage your assets and be sure your best interests are protected. In your most vulnerable moments, you can say you took charge, removed those tough decisions away from your family, and made your family's life easier.

Life Insurance

"Life insurance is a love letter written in dollars."

Marya Mannes, American Author

It is quite easy to underestimate the value of life insurance. Like creating an estate plan, it can be another reminder of your own mortality. Life insurance, however, is essential to the overall health of your family and business finances. It is imperative to make sure you have enough life insurance to take care of all that you planned for you and your family. We can help you analyze your liabilities, your goals and what you want to accomplish, but ultimately, you are the one that needs to make that determination. Perhaps you want to make sure all of your kids are able to go to college even if something happens to you. You want to make sure that can still happen and can still be a viable situation. Life insurance is also a protected asset which can provide protection to your estate.

CONCLUSION

The 3 Bucket Method is a proven system to protect your assets in the real world. This system has been implemented in many trucking businesses to provide the maximum protection to the owners. It is not a magic bullet that makes you invincible (nothing can do that), but rather a system that compartmentalizes risk to minimize your personal exposure and loss. This system can help the trucking business owner who wants to protect what they have worked so hard for. You must commit to maintaining the system for it to continue to provide you with its protection and reduce your risk of loss. Until you take the first step, you are at risk of losing all you have earned up to this point and into the future.

If you have a trucking business that you currently operate, or if you are considering starting out in the trucking business, I hope this book has been a source of information and guidance on how to set up your business structures, or how to make adjustments to your current structure to maximize your asset protection and minimize your tax and other liabilities.

If you find this information useful you can check out our other resources on our YouTube

Channel, The Solution Point; or you can reach us at our websites DickersonLaw.com and DickersonLawCentralTX.com.

Contact us today for your appointment to take the first step in protecting your business and start implementing The 3 Bucket Method in your Trucking Business before it is too late. Call us today by dialing us at 956-791-5422.

This educational book has been provided by The J.M. Dickerson Law Firm PLLC.

Other Titles Available from the Author:

PRINT VERSIONS

The Road Map to Rich, A Lawyers Perspective on Getting and Staying Rich.

The Three Bucket Method for Asset Protection

El Método de las 3 Cubetas Para la Protección de Activos

The Texan's Guide to The Probate Process

Request a copy by calling 956-791-5422.

Social Media Pages

YouTube
https://www.youtube.com/@thesolutionpointwithJMD
Laredo Website
https://dickersonlaw.com
New Braunfels Website
https://www.dickersonlawcentraltx.com
Laredo Facebook
https://www.facebook.com/JMDlaw
New Braunfels Facebook
https://www.facebook.com/JMDlawCentralTX
Instagram
https://www.instagram.com/thejmdlawfirm
LinkedIn
https://www.linkedin.com/in/thejmdlawfirm

Electronic Resources

JMD's Guide to Lasting Peace of Mind EP Workbook	https://www.dickersonlaw.com/estate-planning
Texan's Guide of the Probate Process eBook	https://www.dickersonlaw.com/probate-guardianships
The 3 Bucket Method for Asset Protection eBook	https://www.dickersonlaw.com/business-entity-formation
LMCA Presentación de El Método	https://youtu.be/NefZGznjAfg
Rotary Presentation of Three Bucket Method	https://youtu.be/fQ_Mhzs8v-s
Grow Yourself Video w/ David Kash Vasquez	https://youtu.be/8g0Tw9GKGG4

The 3 Bucket Method
For Asset Protection
For The Trucking Industry

Made in the USA
Monee, IL
04 November 2026

67387510R00085